Crabapples

Celebrating the Powwow

Bobbie Kalman

Crabtree Publishing Company

Crabapples

created by Bobbie Kalman

For Ramona
Welcome to the family!

Editor-in-Chief
Bobbie Kalman

Research
April Fast

Writing team
Bobbie Kalman
Petrina Gentile

Managing editor
Lynda Hale

Editors
Petrina Gentile
Niki Walker
Greg Nickles

Consultants
Kiera L. Ladner;
Jackie Labonte, Niagara
Regional Native Center

Computer design
Lynda Hale
Lucy DeFazio

Special thanks to
Kiera L. Ladner, Jackie Labonte, Burt Anderson, Christina Doyle, and Lance Johnson

Illustrations
Barbara Bedell: page 14, back cover
Darcy Novakowski: pages 9, 19

Photographs
Marc Crabtree: cover, pages 4, 5 (all), 6, 7, 10 (both), 12, 17, 18 (left),
    20, 21, 22 (top), 23, 25 (top), 27 (top left, bottom), 28-29, 30 (both)
Lynda Hale: page 19 (left)
Bobbie Kalman: page 15 (all)
Diane Payton Majumdar: pages 22 (bottom), 27 (top right)
Fred Mercnik: title page, pages 24, 25 (bottom), 26 (right)
Tom Stack and Associates: W. Perry Conway: page 11;
    J. Lotter: page 13; Bob Pool: pages 8, 19 (right); John Shaw: page 31;
    Tom Stack: pages 18 (right), 26 (left); Steve Elmore: page 16

Printer
Worzalla Publishing Company

Color separations and film
Dot 'n Line Image Inc.

Crabtree Publishing Company

350 Fifth Avenue
Suite 3308
New York
N.Y. 10118

360 York Road, RR 4,
Niagara-on-the-Lake,
Ontario, Canada
L0S 1J0

73 Lime Walk
Headington
Oxford OX3 7AD
United Kingdom

Cataloging in Publication Data
Kalman, Bobbie
    Celebrating the Powwow
(Crabapples)
Includes index.
ISBN 0-86505-640-4 (library bound)   ISBN 0-86505-740-0 (pbk.)
This book introduces the peoples, cultures, beliefs, and events
that are a part of many powwows.

1. Powwows - Juvenile literature. 2. Indians of North America
- Rites and ceremonies I. Title. II. Series: Kalman, Bobbie.
Crabapples.
E98.P86K35 1997   j394   LC 97-2107
                                        CIP

What is in this book?

Powwow	4
Many cultures	7
The powwow trail	9
Getting ready	10
The powwow begins	12
Musical instruments	14
Drumming and singing	17
Children at the powwow	19
Men's regalia	20
Women's regalia	22
Dancing	25
Competitions	28
Other events	30
Words to know & Index	32

Powwow

A powwow is a colorful event that involves dancing and drumming. It is the oldest North American celebration. Powwows are held throughout the United States and Canada. They can take place indoors, but most are held outdoors.

The First Nations people gather to celebrate their individual cultures and shared beliefs. Ojibwe, Micmac, Blackfoot, Mohawk, Lakota, and Navajo are the names of some First Nations.

People come to the powwows to meet relatives and friends from other parts of the country—and they come to dance! Hundreds of spectators also flock to the powwows because powwows are lots of fun!

Many cultures

Culture refers to the customs and beliefs of a group of people. There are hundreds of cultures among the First Nations. Their languages and traditions may be different, but many Nations share similar beliefs and values.

One of these beliefs is that all living things are sacred. The turtle and eagle are very important to the First Nations people. They call North America "Turtle Island." In many stories, the turtle plays a large part in the creation of the world. That is why powwow outfits often have turtle designs sewn on them.

The eagle is believed to be the messenger of the Great Spirit. Eagle feathers stand for wisdom. If an eagle feather falls from a costume, the dancers form a circle of protection around it. Everyone is silent. An elder recites a prayer, picks up the feather, and returns it to its owner with a reminder to take care of such a sacred object.

The circle is also very important. It is the shape of many things in nature such as the sun, moon, and earth. Even the seasons form a circle as they change each year. At a powwow, dances are performed inside a circle of spectators, and the drummers sit in a circle as they play.

The powwow trail

People of all ages travel from one powwow to another. The powwow trail, however, is not just the journey people make from powwow to powwow. It is also a journey people make inside their heart and mind. It is a way for each person to strengthen his or her beliefs and values. People do not make this journey only during a powwow. They make it every day of their life. To many people, the powwow trail is a way of life.

Getting ready

There is a lot to do to prepare for a powwow. Family members help one another get dressed. There are several parts to each dance outfit.

Mothers and grandmothers spend many hours embroidering, beading, and doing quillwork to make the fancy designs and patterns on the outfits. Each Nation has its own design and traditional patterns of beading. A person from one Nation can identify another person's Nation just by looking at the beadwork on his or her outfit.

Many people prepare to camp at the powwow. Some Plains Nations people put up tepees in a circle. In the past, the Plains Nations used tepees as their homes because they are easy to carry and put together.

11

The powwow begins

The **grand entry** takes place at the beginning of the powwow. An elder leads a line of dancers and singers into the dance area.

A circle is formed. Once everyone has entered the circle, the elder recites a prayer and welcome speech. He or she places four flags to represent the four directions. These flags vary in color among some Nations, but to many, white is north, yellow is east, red is south, and black or dark blue is west.

A flag song is sung during this part of the ceremony. At some powwows, the National Anthem is also sung.

At some powwows, **princesses** are among the first people to join the grand entry. A princess is a young girl who wins a pageant to represent her Nation for a year. She proudly wears a banner and the outfit of her Nation at different powwows. Choosing princesses is a custom that began with the First Nations of western North America. The young girls below are princesses.

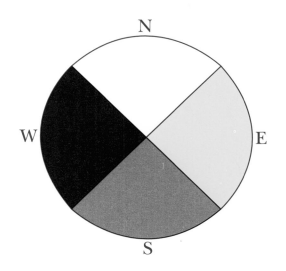

Musical instruments

Music is a big part of the powwow, and the drum is the main instrument. To First Nations people, the drum is sacred. Its sound represents the heartbeat of each Nation and Mother Earth. Different kinds of drums are played at a powwow. A **powwow drum** is a large drum made from the hide of a deer, elk, or horse.

When the drum is not being used, it is covered with a blanket out of respect.

Other musical instruments also have special meanings. The whistle and flute sound like the wind. The rattle is a symbol of hail. Its sound also reminds people of the cricket and rattlesnake.

A **water drum** is a drum that has water in it. The drum is made from a tree trunk, and water is used to moisten the leather **skin**, or lid. The skin comes off the drum so that water can be added or removed. The drum's sound is changed by tightening or loosening the skin.

Making a drum

The pictures below show how one type of hand drum is made. 1. The drum makers first choose the hoop, a long piece of wood that has been steamed and bent into a circle. 2. They spray the hide they have chosen with water and place the hoop over it. 3. They poke holes along the edge of the hide and stretch long, thin strips of hide, or **thongs**. 4. They weave the thongs through the holes around the edge of the hide and then tie two more across the back as a handhold.

handhold

Drumming and singing

A powwow has many drum groups. Each one has a head singer that leads the songs. The drummers sing along as they play. The main drum group, or **host drum**, is chosen by the Nations attending the powwow. Being chosen as the host drum is a great honor.

There is a different song for each type of dance. Some songs are sung with words and others with **vocables**. Vocables are vowel sounds that are repeated, such as "weyaheyeh, weyaheyeh." Some songs have both vocables and words.

Children at the powwow

Powwows are not just for adults. Children participate, too! They take part in dance competitions and can even win prizes! At a powwow, children also play with old friends and meet new ones. They can learn about the cultures and dances of other Nations. Children have a lot of fun at powwows!

Men's regalia

The outfit, or **regalia**, worn by a male dancer differs from one Nation to another. It also differs according to the dance the man is performing.

The regalia shown on page 21 is one type of **traditional** powwow outfit. It shows different parts of a man's regalia. The outfits worn by fancy dancers are more colorful than the traditional outfits. They often include a second bustle.

There are several types of **headdresses**. A **bonnet** is a feather headdress. It hangs from the top of the man's head and down his back in a double row of feathers. A **roach** is made of porcupine quills or horsehair and has many feathers in the center. Some headdresses are masks that represent animals, but not all Nations wear masks.

headddress (roach)

headdress
(bonnet)

bustle

necklace

shirt yoke

fringes

dancing stick trimmed
with eagle feathers

breastplate

wristband
or gauntlet

sash

apron

full-length
leggings

Moccasins are made of animal
hide and fit like a soft slipper.
Some are lined with fur to keep
the feet warm. They are often
decorated with beads.

Women's regalia

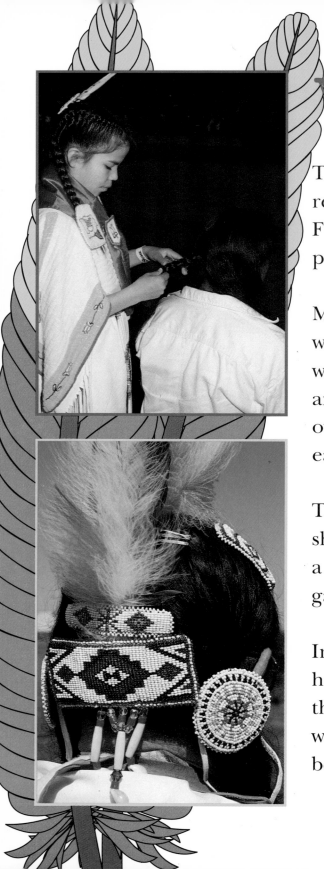

The designs and patterns on women's regalia vary from one Nation to another. Female dancers wear various outfits to perform different types of dances.

Many powwow outfits are embroidered with quills and elaborate beads. Some women wear a shawl over their outfit, and others do not. Some carry a shawl over their arm. Some women carry an eagle-feather fan, and others do not.

The woman's traditional outfit, shown on the next page, can include a dress, skirt, shawl, moccasins, gauntlets, and leggings.

In the past, women and men wore their hair in braids. Today, many still braid their hair, but some wear it short. Both women and men adorn their hair with beads or feathers.

woman's traditional powwow outfit

collar

medallion

cape

eagle-feather fan

necklace

wristband
or gauntlet

breastplate
with beadwork

shawl

beaded purse

dress

ribbon

Underneath the
dress, there is a skirt
and leggings that
reach the knees.

moccasin

23

Dancing

There are many kinds of dances at a powwow. Some dances are performed by men only, and others are danced by women only. Some are danced by men and women of the same Nation, and others are open to people of all Nations.

When people from many different Nations dance together non-competitively, the dance is called an **inter-tribal** dance. The first and last dances performed at a powwow are always inter-tribal dances. The dancers move around the circle in a clockwise or counter-clockwise direction. The direction depends on the tradition of the Nation in whose territory the powwow is being held.

Fancy dances are livelier than **traditional dances**. Fancy dancers wear feathers that have been dyed in bright colors such as red and yellow. Some use metallic beads, sequins, and ribbons and wear two bustles instead of one.

The Shawl Dance, above, is a woman's fancy dance. A woman wears a shawl over her shoulders. She holds its ends with her hands. The shawl flies around while the dancer jumps and turns to the fast drumbeat, but it must never touch the ground!

The Hoop Dance is a fancy dance for men. The dancer spins hoops on his arms and legs. Some say the hoops symbolize the "circle of life."

In the Grass Dance, dancers stomp their feet as if to flatten grass for a campsite. In the past, grass dancers wore sweet grass in their belts. As they moved, it swayed like grass in the wind. Today's "grass" is made of ribbons and yarn.

The Jingle Dress Dance is a lively dance for girls and women. When the dancer moves her feet to the fast beat of the drum, the cone-shaped bells on her outfit jingle to the music.

Competitions

Some of the dances at a powwow are contests. Dancers compete in five categories: tiny tots (ages 1-5), juvenile (6-12), junior (13-17), senior (18-49), and golden age (over 50).

Children love to dance in the competitions. Most perform fancy dances. Golden-age dancers, on the other hand, usually perform traditional dances.

Dancers work hard to do their very best. They are judged on their moves, outfits, and how well they know the music. They must be sure to stop dancing exactly on the last beat of the drum. If they do not, they lose points.

Dancers can win a lot of money if they dance well. It is fun to win money, but most dancers are happy to win because they are proud of their dance skills and the culture to which they belong.

Other events

Although dancing is a big part of a powwow, there are many other events. Most powwows have arts-and-crafts displays and food stalls.

At some powwows, fashion shows feature modern designs in Native clothing. Sometimes singers perform and authors read aloud.

At the end of many powwows, there is an event called a **giveaway**. It involves the traditions of sharing and honoring. People are honored for helping organize the powwow or doing good deeds in their community. Gifts for drummers, elders, or dancers are sometimes laid out on a blanket. In another type of giveaway, a girl is given a shawl to welcome her as a new powwow dancer. Traditionally, a powwow ends with an **honor song** and a prayer for a safe journey.

Words to know

embroidery The art of stitching fancy designs with a needle and thread

fancy dance A dance based on traditional dance but performed in more colorful costumes and using livelier steps

First Nations The original inhabitants of North America and their descendants; Blackfoot and Micmac are examples

Great Spirit The god worshipped by many First Nations people

honor song A song sung at the end of a powwow as a sign of respect and pride

powwow trail The physical journey from powwow to powwow; also considered a way of life by many First Nations people

procession A line of people moving in an orderly manner, as in a ceremony

quillwork Decorative work done with the quills or spines of a porcupine or hedgehog

regalia An outfit that includes special emblems and symbols

sacred An object that is respected because of its association with a religion or god

tradition The knowledge, beliefs, and customs that are passed from one generation to the next

traditional costume An outfit based on tradition

traditional dance A dance performed in the style of original First Nation dances

Index

beading 10, 21, 22, 23, 26
circle 7, 10, 12, 15, 25, 27
children 13, 19, 27, 28, 31
competitions 19, 28
cultures 4, 7, 9, 19, 28
customs 7, 13
dancing 4, 7, 12, 17, 19, 20, 21, 22, 25-27, 28, 30, 31
drum making 15
drumming 4, 7, 14, 17, 26, 27, 28, 31
eagle 7
elders 7, 10, 12, 28, 31

embroidering 10, 22
feathers 7, 20, 21, 22, 23, 26
First Nations 4, 7, 10, 12, 13, 14, 17, 19, 20, 22, 25
flags 12
friends 4, 19
giveaway *see* other events
grand entry 12-13
hair 22
headdresses 20, 21
masks 20
moccasins 21, 22, 23
music 14-15, 27, 28

other events 30-31
outfits *see* regalia
powwow trail 9
prayers 7, 12, 31
preparing for a powwow 10
princesses 13
quillwork 10, 20, 22
regalia 7, 10, 13, 20-23, 26, 27, 28
relatives 4, 10
singing 12, 17, 30, 31
spectators 4, 7
Turtle Island 7

1 2 3 4 5 6 7 8 9 0 Printed in USA 6 5 4 3 2 1 0 9 8 7